diamond and graphite

gopika kohli

Invincible Publishers

First published in India in 2019

ISBN: 978-93-88333-91-7

Registered Address: 201A, SAS Tower, Sector 38, Gurgaon-122003

Printed at Thomson Press (India) LTD

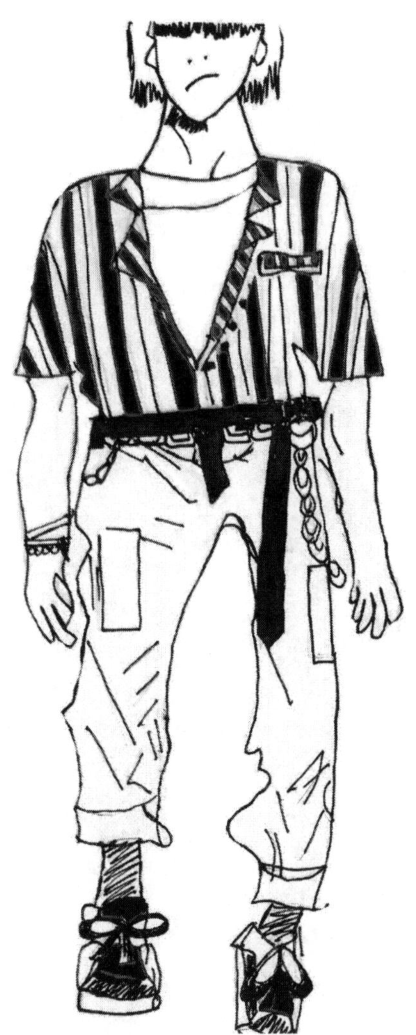

acknowledgement

I would like to thank myself for facing my fears and jotting down my emotions. Without that, I would never have been able to express myself in my poetry.

I would like to thank Rupi Kaur for introducing me to the art of poetry and capturing what one feels and express it openly. I would like to thank Ma for reading and analysing each of my pieces and giving her honest opinions. I would like to thank my dad for his presence and support in whatever I have ever wished to do. I would like to thank Sonali for being my depression doodle partner and appreciating my unusual art. I would like to thank Sameera for the support. I would like to thank my other friends for being the context and reason I write.

about the title

Diamond and graphite are two products from the same allotropes. Same material but different dimensions. One is considered the most precious stone whereas the other is the most ordinary one. Human beings are also made up of happiness and sadness. The person is determined by which feature of their personality they wish to showcase to others. That's what holds their value. The contradicting perspective makes you wonder what you are.

table of contents

I AM LOST
I AM LOST
I AM LOST
I AM LOST
HELP ME

/ dichotomy of Life

There's a time
When the rays don't shine anymore
And your life seems dull

There's a time
When you feel like the clock ticking
And your life is drifting away

There's a time
When you don't want this anymore
When you want to be alone

There's a time
When you want to feel loved
When you hate them all

There's a time
When you want to cry your heart out
When all you want is silence

There's a time
When you want to be pretty
And want to be ugly too

There's a time
When clouds feel angelic
But rain washes your sorrows

There's a time
When humans feel grand
But they are the only threat

There's a time
When you feel like trash
But it holds your secrets

There's a time
When you love yourself
But still want to be some one else

There's a time
When the darkness frightens you
But stars fascinate you

There's a time
When the sun feel too bright
But it only lights your life

There's a time
When you don't want anything
And everything is needed

There's a time
When everything seems good
and that's what troubles you

There's a time
When you want to kill yourself
And that only terrifies you

There's a time
When you want to let it all out
Cause its killing you inside

There's a time
When angels bring peace
But devils feel realistic

There's a time
When you feel your heart beating
Also when it turns stone cold

there's a time
when these seams seen ugly
when they only bring peace

there's a time
when family is the worst thing on earth
when they only bring comfort

there's a time
when questions flood your head
and aren't there when needed

there's a time
when life is all that matters
and death feel good

there's a time
when escape is needed
and thats the only trap

there's a time
when clothes feel nice
and you want to rip them off

There is a time
when you feel high
but you only take yourself down

There is a Time... There is a Time...There is a Time

/ shattered

i am a piece of glass
close to getting shattered
on the verge of breaking
with each harmful word you say
i chip some more

i don't know how long
this glass is going to sustain
before it breaks
and how long can i keep pretending to be
who i am not

I DON'T
KNOW WHAT
I'M DOING
WITH MY
LIFE

/ tell me your story

tell me your story
tell me what you are going through

tell me about the times
you have suffered
tell me about the times
you were numb with pain
when you wanted to howl
but no tears came
when you wanted to burst
but were shunned by the maddening silence

tell me about the times
when you didn't fit in
about times
when you felt isolated from everyone around you
about the times
when you didn't want to face reality because you were too engrossed in your fantasy world

tell me about the times
when you gave up on something you wanted
about the times

you gave up on your dreams
due to logical reasoning of the people
when you gave up on your happiness
for someone else's happiness
when you were afraid
to do something you wanted to do,
something you wanted
but were scared about everyone's view

tell me about the long arguments
you have been a part of
the times when you had to defend yourself
when everyone was against you
when you had to defend yourself
because of your actions
because everyone thought they were wrong.

tell me about your stories
every single one of them
because once you are done
i have my own stories awaiting to be told

/ happiness

happiness
is something everyone is taught
but is it worth it,
to smile
while you are breaking inside?
to help others
when you can't seem to understand what's wrong with
you
to laugh
when it's the most difficult task in the world.
is it worth it?
is it worth it to put up an act
to escape the wrath of the society
who would otherwise
question and question
your rebellious action?

IS LIFE REALLY BEAUTIFUL?

/ depression

depression
my depression ruins me
day by day
taking away all i longed and desired

replacing them with endless tears and sorrows.
i have lost count of the times
when i have pitied myself
when i just couldn't do anything
when i couldn't get out of the bed
when i just couldn't stop crying.

my depression has destroyed me
has changed everything around me
the concerned and worried faces are gone
switched to utter disgust and shame towards me
emptying me...more and more
day by day.

drowned so deep
there is no escape
my loneliness became my best friend
oblivious to the rest
my depression takes the best of me
leaves the worst to me

i grow weaker by each voice
giving up my thoughts, actions, my voice, myself.

i have lost everything
i have lost faith in things
i have stopped trying to feel happy
emotions and i don't get along anymore
my depression has spoiled my relations
more, the relation with myself

my depression has ended things
my depression has ended moments for me
my depression has ended my relations for me
my depression has ended my desires
my depression has ended my life
all so slowly, oblivious to everyone, oblivious to myself

/ mother

all i needed was
a touch of grace

to make this sorrowful creature
lively again

tried finding it everywhere
don't know where it hides

wish i had always known
it was beside me always

angel of god
devil in its worst form

a mother,
a blessing who loves you more than herself
and also makes you work more than herself

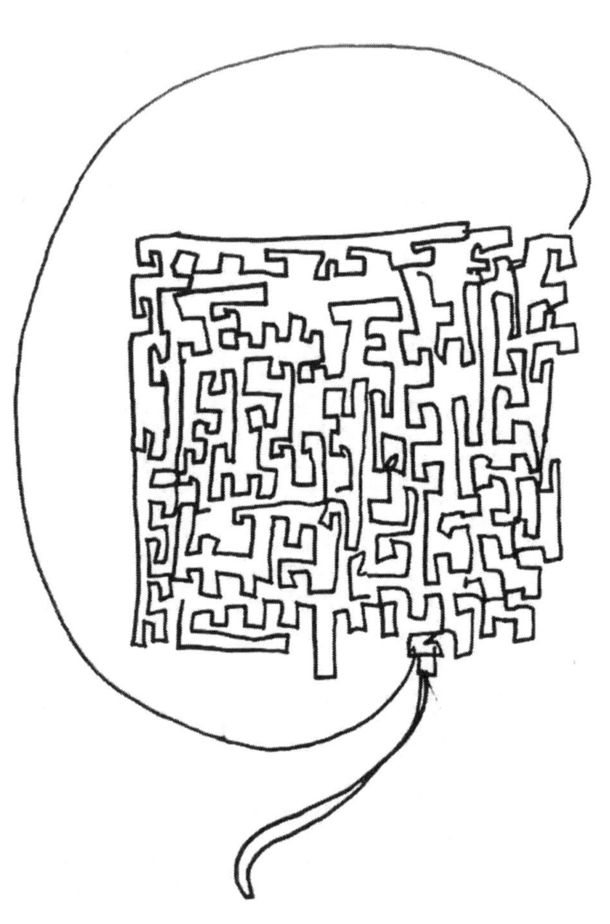

/ emptiness

what is it that the heart desires?
what is it that it wants from the world?

why does it long for something
something which is unknown?
what is that something?
why does it seem so near
yet so far?

disappointed, sunken, broken
why am i feeling this way?
what have i seem to have lost
of which i am not aware?

what is this mess
which i have created
but not able to clear?

where is my mind?
what am i doing?
why isn't anything making sense?

why, why, why, why
why am i loosing myself to the world?

i have suffered through something,
something reckless

which in the end makes you
feel restless
makes you feel hopeless
you can't escape this
feeling

we have all tried
the harder you try to deny it
the further you fall
the feeling isn't to unknown
this feeling is emptiness

/ have you?

have you ever wondered
how it would feel to have everything you have ever desired?

to touch everything you have dreamed of touching
discover things you have always been wondering
going to all the places you did not even know about
craving all there is in this world
starting of the adventure you have always dreamed about
imagining all the circumstances you didn't know about
feeling emotions which you thought you could never feel
the challenges you never thought existed
the eternal happiness which you thought wasn't possible
the love which you never received

have you ever wondered how you would feel the life
you have always wanted to live?

have you?

The phases keep
on changing...
but I
but I
still remain the
same.

/ bothered

broken
shattered
thrown away

numb
cold
escape? no way

unworthy
useless
does everyone feels this way?

happy
glowing
i want to feel special in some way!

is there anything which can be done?
or should i...or should i
stop feeling bothered by such a way?

/ strangers

the people she thought she knew,
turned out to be strangers

the paper she thought was blank
turned out to be rubbed till nothing was there

the story she thought was complete,
it didn't have any ending

the song she really liked,
now doesn't make her feel anything.

all that seemed to be good,
is tumbling down now

she was taught...
she was taught to stay strong no matter what happens,

she was taught...
she was taught not to let her walls fall

all these changes, all these new things,
made her realise...
made her realise
she didn't belong here

/ no strength

the shadow of the kite
lies right at the tip
of where i am standing

feeling unsure
not so safe
full of insecurity

my fears take the best of me
and keep the worst to me

slowly, slowly i am drifting away
not so sure, why I am feeling this way

!! no strength !!

full of negativeness
why negativity, why had the way!
why so unsure of what to say

tears break down
body lies down

!! no strength !!

cry, cry myself a river
to drown my sorrows in them

to bring up my self esteem
which leads to me breaking down

but alas

!! no strength !!

/ guilt

the feeling of guilt
is the worst of them all

it starts its mission
and takes small steps
but it does not stop till the whole body
is drowning in this feeling

it gets better they all say
they have been through this
they all know it doesn't get better
but no one would want to push you further down

the feeling of guilt
is the trickiest of them all
you try to escape it
but its already two steps ahead
waiting for you to come back
waiting for you to experience it all again
and again
and again

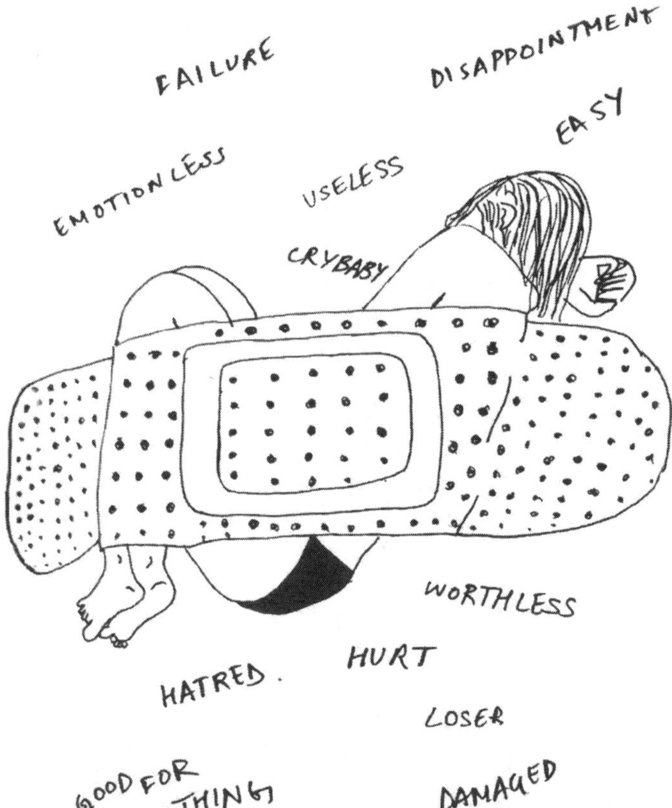
DISAPPOINTMENT
FAILURE
EASY
EMOTIONLESS
USELESS
CRYBABY
WORTHLESS
HURT
HATRED.
LOSER
GOOD FOR
NOTHING
DAMAGED

/ hurt

i sometimes wonder
why do i do this?
why do i try my very best to ruin someone's day
when it's not even my main intention, not my main
motive

it's like negativity is filled in my vein
sorrow in my soul
and my body is electrified with hatred

i try to escape it
i try not to drown but the more i struggle to free myself
from this trap
the more i fail

the more people i target
the more people i disappoint
the more people i hurt

the more i drown in the feeling of guilt

/ when

when will you stop calling
when will your heart stop hurting
when you think about your past memories

when will your eyes stop watering
at the mention of anything from your past

when will you be able to face reality
when will you be able to accept what had happened

when will you be able to stop hiding and live again

when will the sadness pass
when will you be able to do
whatever it is that you have dreamt about
without putting your heart on strings?

/ almighty

you made us believe in ourselves
when we thought we weren't capable of

you made us follow our dreams
when we couldn't reach them

you made us bear the pain
when it was too much to handle

you made us successful
when we ourselves had lost hope

you made us put on a smile
when we were breaking down inside

you made us fight negativity
by filling us with positivity

you introduced us to hope
when our minds weren't working

you made us think it was right
when it all felt wrong

you make life so easy
when it feels like a burden

you make us feel loved
when the universe is against us

you made us feel confident
when we were on the edge of giving up

you were always present
when we ourselves weren't sure of

you showed us light
when we thought we were filled with darkness

you made us feel satisfied
when we didn't have anything

you made us feel alive
when we were dying inside

you helped everyone
even if they were against you

you connected people
and made them a family

you made everyone believe
we are the same

you made us feel united and equal

you, almighty
are the greatest thing
and the most magical mystery ever

/ the book

a book which is filled with mystery
a book which everyone likes

either has one story or another
with different plots and characters

it keeps us occupied
by building a maze in your mind

it either fascinates or confuses you
till you can't handle it anymore

but still we keep on going
and imagining every step we take

which can land us in an explanation
or put us in a war zone

only one mastermind is behind
who knows every answer to this

oh you author
your book is divine

THE ART OF *letting go*

LEAVE
LEAVE LEAVE
LEAVE
LEAVE LEAVE
LEAVE LEAVE
LEAVE LEAVE LEAVE
LEAVE LEAVE
LEAVE LEAVE
LEAVE LEAVE
LEAVE LEAVE
LEAVE LEAVE

/ start living

can there be a word search
to help me identify who I am?
everyone wants us to be who they desire
what about our desires?

everyone is disappointed in us
what about us?
who are we disappointed in?

they say we make ourselves insane
isn't that what the voices also say?

they say we hurt their feelings.
do they even know what they are?

do this, do that, be this, be that
why can't i just be myself?

'don't worry, be happy'
embrace your weirdness
stop labelling start living

ANGEL OR
DEVIL

IN THE END
YOU R
HUMAN

&

HUMANS
SUCK

/ righteousness

sometimes i wonder
am i right or am i right
or am i wrong as they say?

this world is a cruel place
no place for the 'wrong people'

try to find a place
try to be right
'fail unpleasantly'

what are we?
what am i?
why am i labelled as 'wrong' i wonder?

is it my nature? is it my attitude? or is it the way i am?

yes, says the world, yes, says the society
no, says my heart
it's your uniqueness
its them who feel that you
are the so called 'wrong'
they are the ones who are wrong!!

WHO AM I?

WHO WAS I BEFORE SOCIETY SHAPED ME?

AM I HAPPY?

AXZYL MNS QR..

/ stuck

a sudden flashback
brought her back to the real world
the world she feared
the world she wanted to escape from

all her memories
trapped her
and none of her loved ones
could make her escape it

she became hollow,
fragile,
filled with terror and fright

she couldn't escape her mind
all those experiences
which made her feel
unworthy,
useless
couldn't go away
they kept coming back
kept trapping her back

she lost hope
to be happy again
to live again
or even realise that all had passed
and she was still stuck on the same page

How does one realize what he truly wants?

Do you sometimes feel that the actions which you want to take will have bad consequences and thus you stick with what the others desire of you?

Every day do you lose ample time from your small life going against what you want to do because you are afraid you won't have an answer when people demand it from you.

You start letting people be the storytellers of your life, directing you regarding what steps to take, why and where. Don't do this. Be the architect of your life and experience mistakes too. You start living the fantasy bubble about your life which everyone else expects you to be in and have a gala time too!

Stop. Stop allowing people to take your life away from you. Stop not following your dreams. Stop getting scared of getting judged. Breathe. What is meant to happen will anyway.

Self-love isn't selfish.

If you aren't fully satisfied with what you are, don't love the way you are, don't appreciate your own choices, you will never be able to give your 100% to someone else.

Caring about one's own self and making the decisions you want isn't selfish, it's a necessity.

Don't start hating yourself due to the judgements of others, you can't always satisfy people around you and you shouldn't even strive for anything like this.

Make your own choices, make yourself proud. In this lifetime the longest relationship you have is with yourself, don't damage it for someone else. Love yourself, tell yourself you are worth it and you will get through everything. Make this your motto. You only got one life, live it the way you want.

Your time in this world is limited whereas the people you meet are unlimited, each person makes you learn a new thing, each memory gives you a new feel and each fight teaches you a new lesson.

We live in a very self-centered and materialistic world today which is fueled by people's selfish needs and desires. People don't care about how others feel. People tend to take advantage of you and portray themselves as victims, feeling used and putting the whole blame on the youth. The world needs better people; people with pure desires and people who care about others and their feelings. You are here for a limited period of time, you don't know when the people whom you love or hate the most is going to go away. Cherish them, love them, value them, don't be burdened by the guilt of your impulsive actions. It's an endless passage, a circle with no end. It keeps on going as long as you live. Don't get stuck at one person, one mistake, one memory; life doesn't wait for anyone, don't be so late that you are never able to catch up again. Move on. Love. Live.

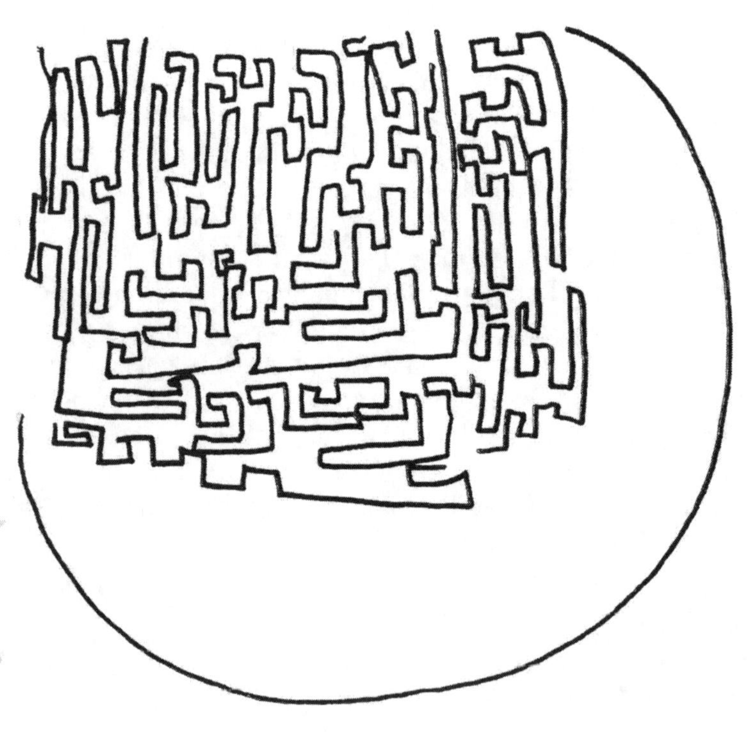

/ human ambition

wind blows
leaves fly

clouds rain
rivers flow

mystery of nature
god knows

he, the destructor
us creatures

in all simplicity
we ruin them

this madness keeps on going
we keep on howling

coz this destruction
results in us breaking

slowly, slowly, slowly

dreams dreams dreams dreams dream
dreams dreams dreams dreams dream
dreams dreams dreams dreams
dreams dreams dreams dreams
dreams dreams dreams dreams
dreams dreams dreams dreams dreams
dreams dreams dreams
dreams dreams dreams
dreams dreams dreams dreams
dreams dreams dreams
dreams dreams dreams
dreams dreams dreams dreams dream
dreams dreams dreams dreams
dreams dreams dreams dreams
dreams dreams dream dreams
dreams dreams dreams dreams
dreams dreams dreams dreams dreams
dreams dreams dreams dreams
dreams dreams dreams dreams
dreams dreams dreams dreams dream
dreams dreams dreams dream dreams
dreams dreams dreams dreams dream
dreams dreams dreams dreams dreams
dreams dreams dreams dreams dreams

/ dream

her body shimmered
along with the soft melody

she was floating
with every movement

this was her cure
from the world so impure

where people were rampageous
and everyone billowing

the deep silence
brought her relief and made sense

rather than shouting obnoxiously
on top of our voices

while working
she kept herself abreast
to her dancing

this was her dream
a dream which she will never be able to achieve

/ heaven

a place
covered and deserted

no one goes there
no animals neither humans

no footsteps
outside or in

no one takes the risk
to go there and be strangled

who knows which creature
how strange and rampageous

but no one knew
that a beautiful lake shined
white doves flew

it is enchanting
but no one can take this risk
to see this magical mist

/ love

i have suffered through something

something reckless

which makes you feel restless

makes you feel hopeless

you can't escape this feeling

we have all tried

the harder you try to deny it, the further you fall

this feeling isn't too unknown

this feeling is love

#metoo

/ justice

her screams muffled
her lips trembling
cries ignored
a state of hopelessness

the injustice against her was brutal
her body disfigured
her confidence shattered
her life ruined

six times over, six times the pain
six times the disgust
lust stricken desire
shattering the life
not of one, but all females of the country

they were made to realise
their body was not a piece of art
their body was an object
made to fulfil
the hunger of sex driven males

the males we gave birth to
whom we nurture
whom we taught
they forgot we weren't toys
but humans with feelings too

the nation yet again failed
to provide security
to provide equality
'bharat mata' our goddess
only turned against us

/ friends

friends
they are like flowers.
in the beginning they look beautiful and
they attract you towards them;
just like pollen attracts insects
but as soon as the purpose is over
they leave you

friend are like roses
everyone likes them
everyone wants them
but in the end,
the thorns do prick you

friends are like seasons
they come and go
friends are like a fashion trend
few like them and try to use them
in their lives, others just don't get them

/ terrorism - the ugly face

god made us all equal
then why such injustice?

one minute someone is alive
and the next, we hear he has died

why does sorrow fill our pores
when happiness can take us all home?

humans, why be so cruel
and have no feelings at all?

life is enchanting,
a journey
that everyone should ride
and not run and hide

happiness to be present in every shred
not covered entirely with bloodshed

humanity is required
terrorism isn't

be humane
stop giving us nightmares

living
in
a
bubble

/ not my cup of tea

head spinning
words mixing
everything is a puzzle

maths problem
a code to track
no detective can do

what are all these rules
is it a textbook or a rule book

ouch it hurts
oops its wrong

what to do
what not to

how to figure out
what to find

math you seriously are a mystery

WHATS FUNNY?

/ science or english

my mind is wondering
what to do?

to take up science
or leave it too

i like science
science hates me

what is this?
god help me!

my brain says science
but my heart, english

why can't you both decide
and not involve me in your problem?

i ain't einstien
i ain't shakespeare

i am me
and that's what i want to be

oh my future
tell me what to do

should i sit here and study
or play ying – yang do

my mind is thinking
what to do

o god, what should i do?
i ain't you too

/ loss

to lose someone
yes everyone who comes in this world has to leave once
his/her time is over

we can make a fuss about it
cry about it
become depressed and be lonely about it

its not going to change the scenario
its just going to change how you see the world and now
you change your mood

remember the time you spent with them, the thoughts, the
laughter, the hard times

everything....
miss them, remember them but don't make yourself sad
about it
think that heaven has got another beautiful angel

look up to the sky and smile at them

make them proud

/ terror

winds were blowing
and the sun was shining bright
cheery feeling all around

no one expected
the leaves to fall
the sky to become dull
an eerie feeling taking place

the mosque was marvellous
it's beauty made it look royal
namaz reciting
reaching everyone's ears

peace

walls full of inscriptions
people reading quran
people praying

no one knew
soon the walls were going to be covered with blood
gun firing would be the only noise that would be heard
motionless bodies would be lying around

families came united
returned divided
some didn’t leave

The mosque no longer
a safe house
rather a grave
with the last voice echoing
‘welcome son’’

"The whole world
in your
hands..."

/ standout

in our entire lifetime
all we do is
try to please everyone
try to fit in
try to make everything alright

while doing all this what we do not realize is that
we lose ourselves
we slowly start to forget who we are
we slowly start breaking down

we slowly lose the touch of our uniqueness

why fit in when you are born to standout!

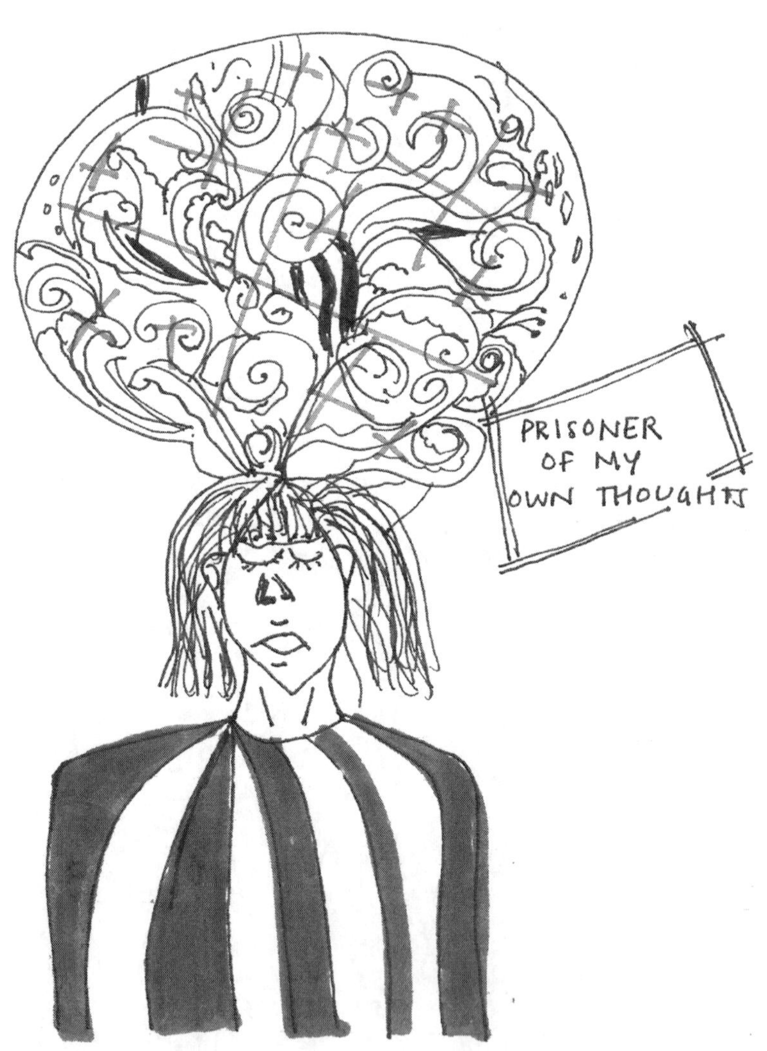
PRISONER
OF MY
OWN THOUGHTS

/ self worth

her soul was filled with regret
regret of wanting, something for herself
regret for demanding a little attention
regret for wanting someone who would care about her
regret for searching a soul she could love

she was made aware that she wasn't worth it
her worth, people had made here realise
but she wasn't ready to accept what was told
to give up her voice
to give up her right to dream

her desire for longing
she wouldn't give it all up
she wouldn't
she knew she was worth it

she deserved everything as much as anyone else
and she knew
that if she gave up
this would be her biggest regret of them all

WHAT AM I?
MIRROR MIRROR
ON THE WALL,
WHAT AM I?
MIRROR MIRROR
ON THE WALL,
WHAT AM I?
MIRROR MIRROR
ON THE WALL,
WHAT AM I?
MIRROR MIRROR,
WHAT AM I?
music

/ you

it was you
whose calls i answered at 2:47 am in the morning

it was you
who used to come in my mind when i would think of
the brightest star every other day

it was you
with who i had shared my fondest memories
and my worst nightmares

it was you
whose fights i turned into mine
and whose battles won were my own victory

it was you
who I showed a part of me
the part unknown to the rest

it was you
whose tears made me forget my own

it was you
whose life was what mattered
but for whom mine was irrelevant

it was you
and your sorrows
i would spend the whole day worrying

it was you
who became my priority
that i forgot anything else existed

it was you
that i left all my own desires for
busy running after yours

it was you
who i believed made me the happiest i had ever been
disarming all the sorrow you had caused

it was you
who at the end of the day
i would return to irrespective of my needs

it was you
whose approval was a necessity for me
i forgot my own self image

it was you
for whom i spent all my time worrying

but,

it was also you
on whom i lost all my tears
the ones you weren't even aware of

it was you
your emotions blinded me
i forgot my own existed

it was you
whose happiness became my problem
leading me to forget the solution to my own

it was you
who i considered an angel
but you were my devil in the worst form

it was you
who i spent hours trying to change
instead you changed me

it was you
who made me the worst possible form of me
only when I was trying my hardest
to make you the best of yours

IS SEPERATION NECESSARY? DO WE HAVE A CHOICE?

/ nature

streams separating
hurling down
crashing again and again
making a grand sound

droplets falling
as melodic as possible
glittering and glistering
touching the ground

clouds banging
creating lightening
we see thunder
in the night, sparkling

at last we attain happiness
we see a rainbow above the blue mountains
wiping the gloominess from our eyes
a twinkling feeling in our eyes

/ kahaani

what is it that you want?
what is it that you like?
why do you ask others
about your story?

tell me your story
tell me your words

what is it that you are scared of?
that it won't be good?
that it won't be like you
imagined it to be?
change it then

it is your story
it is in your own hands

what is it that you are good at?
what is it that you want to do?
what is it in your heart?

tell me
share it
tell the world this is what it is

what are you so afraid of?
what will people say?
show it to them

tell them
it's your story

why keep on copying the
story of others?
same story again and again
make a new one
maybe it will not work
but if it does

it will be your kahaani

/ fruit of life

plant the seed of love
water it with care

through the years
the leaves of feelings will grow
shower them with values

when you have fulfilled your duty
the flower of affection will blossom

receive your fruit of hard work
the sweetest of them all

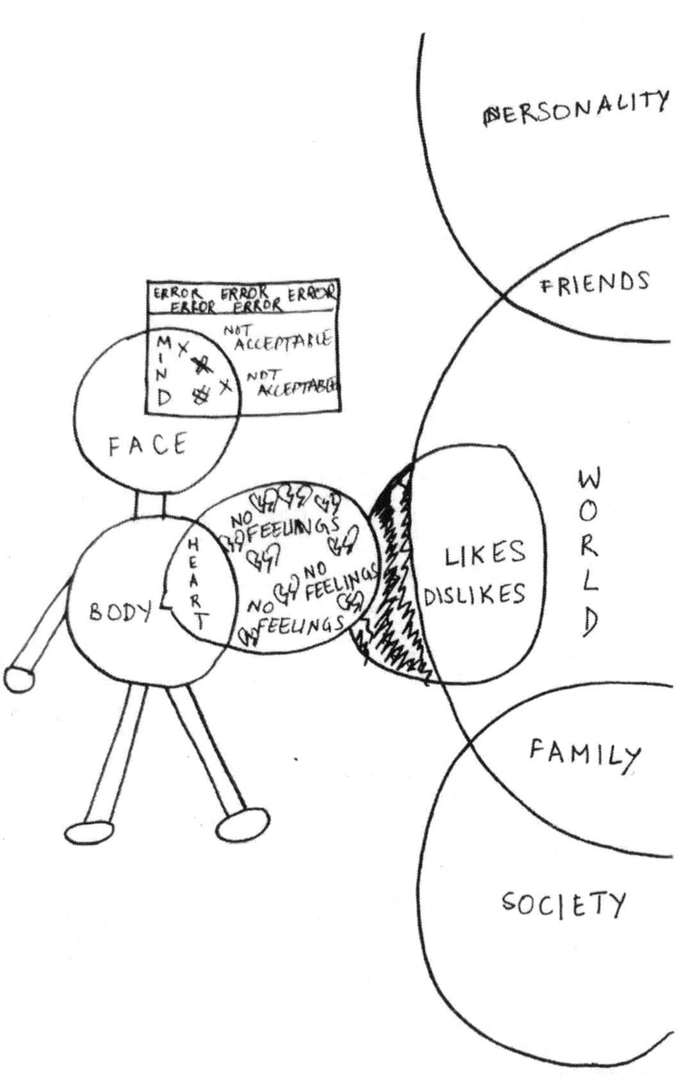

ERROR ERROR ERROR
ERROR ERROR
MIND
NOT ACCEPTABLE
NOT ACCEPTAB
FACE
NO FEELINGS
NO FEELINGS
NO FEELINGS
HEART
BODY
LIKES
DISLIKES
PERSONALITY
FRIENDS
WORLD
FAMILY
SOCIETY

/ why

the water on the flower glistening
why does it look so pretty?

the smile on a child's face
why does it make you happy?

a dog crying out in pain
why does it make you sad?

listening to music
why does it make you feel relaxed?

a lot of homework
why does it make you stressed?

why do these emotions play with our brains?
one moment we are happy, then insane.

why do they describe and express us?
they aren't even living

why do they drive us mad?
why do they make us want to bang our head hard?

why do we meet new people?
why can't the old one's stick?

why do flowers blossom and then die?
why can't they stay like that?

why can't we predict future?
why we only make it?

why this? why that?

why?

/ farewell

it's a sincere request
from my soul and me

sadness
my best friend
it's time for us to go out separate ways
it's time for us to move on

you have been with me
through all my journey
unexpected
but I don't want you anymore

i can't deal with you anymore
i can't burden myself with the weight of you
always on my shoulder
always waiting to come out

i have severed all my ties with people
i have severed the tie with myself
i was too deep into you
i can't be with you anymore

i am sure
that i won't be able to get rid of you
not so easily when you have taken over all my heart
but i have heard you tried

there is nothing which cannot be undone
i am moving on
i am leaving you behind

this is a thought from my heart
i hope you can understand it

it's a goodbye best friend
i hope we never interlink again

/ friday the 13th

winds hurling
bats cackling

eerie sounds
vibrate around

clouds bursting
thunder sparkling

cats crossing
cars racing

frightening us
the red lights

stalls shining bright
sky cloudless

leaves make sounds
as one goes around

its pitch black
don't want to come back

/ when i die

the day i die
a whole burden would be lifted
i will get what i needed my whole life
my freedom

the day i die
a whole burden would be lifted
my family will live its life more freely
there would be no sorrow

the day i die
a whole burden would be lifted
the rainbows and stars would be uplifted,
from the rains and thunder

the day i die
a whole burden would be lifted
my depression would end
it wouldn't destroy everything I love anymore

the day i die
a whole burden would be lifted
the feeling of guilt which is slowly engulfing me
will not succeed

the day i die
a whole burden would be lifted
the shakes of disapproval would end
freeing me of rejection

the day i die
a whole burden would be lifted
it would be the happiest day of my life

about the author

Gopika Kohli is a school student with a zest for life. She took to poetry as a form of expression in 2016. Her poems have been included in books like Triumph of Learning and Hungarian Anthology “A Step Here A Mile There”. She has participated in The Udaipur Literary Fest. She is inspired by Rupi Kaur. A creative person by heart she loves to write, draw doodles, sketch, read and perform. In her poems she writes about the reality of lives we lead; realities which we are mostly ignorant about. She strongly feels that there is no right or wrong way to do poetry and keeps writing what touches her soul.

She has recited her poems at a couple of literary events at both national and international level. She is a contributor to her school magazine and has been an active member of her school’s editorial team.

Her oratory skills helped her get nominated to her School Parliament and she has been effective in establishing a strong communication channel between the students and the faculty in this role. An active volunteer in various teaching programs, sanitation drives and nature conservation activities through school and NGO sponsored initiatives, she believes in giving back to community. Gopika Kohli loves pop music and reading thriller.

She is looking forward to build her career in the field of communication and wishes to pursue formal higher education in this discipline at a reputed school in India or Abroad. She can be found at www.gopikakohli.com.

Diamond and Graphite is her first collection of illustrations and poems.